FARM DOGS

BARNYARD FRIENDS

Jason Cooper

The Rourke Book Co., Inc.
Vero Beach, Florida 32964

Edited by Sandra A. Robinson and Pamela J.P. Schroeder

PHOTO CREDITS
All photos © Lynn M. Stone

Library of Congress Cataloging-in-Publication Data

Cooper, Jason, 1942-
    Farm dogs / by Jason Cooper.
    p. cm. — (Barn yard friends)
    Includes index.
    ISBN 1-55916-091-8
    1. Dogs—Juvenile literature. [1. Dogs. 2. Farm life.]
I. Title. II. Series: Cooper, Jason, 1942- Barn yard friends.
SF426.5.C68   1995
636.7'0886—dc20   94-39534
                                                            CIP
                                                            AC

Printed in the USA

TABLE OF CONTENTS

FARM DOGS

More than 50 million dogs live in North America. Those that live on farms are farm dogs.

Dogs are loyal, obedient and friendly to kind masters. Long ago they earned the name "man's best friend."

Dogs and their wild cousins — foxes, coyotes, jackals and wolves — belong to a group of meat-eating animals called **carnivores.**

Many breeds make good farm dogs, like this Old English sheepdog

HOW DOGS LOOK

Dogs may be large or small, fat or thin, tall or short. They may be long-haired, short-haired or almost without any hair!

The tiny Chihuahua weighs just four pounds. The great Saint Bernard may weigh 200 pounds. One of the largest Saint Bernards weighed 300 pounds!

Dogs have claws on their toes and sharp teeth like other hunters.

Still popular on farms as a guard dog, the German shepherd is one of the herding dogs

WHERE DOGS LIVE

Nearly every farm seems to have a dog. Many farms have more than one dog.

Farm dogs are outdoor dogs. They usually have their own doghouse and do not go into the farmer's home. Some farm dogs live in barns.

Farms dogs treat the farm as their own property, or **territory.** Sometimes, though, they roam far away from the farm.

A farm becomes a dog's territory

BREEDS OF DOGS

The first "dogs" were probably wolves that people in Europe and Asia caught 12,000 years ago. Over a long period of time with people, these wild dogs became less wolflike.

Each special type became a **breed.** People raised dogs to be different shapes and sizes by carefully picking which dogs to use as mothers and fathers. The American Kennel Club lists 132 breeds. There may be more than 400 breeds around the world.

Most dogs on farms are mixed breeds, also known as mutts or **mongrels.**

The collie, once often used to herd cattle and sheep, is still a farm favorite

11

Trained herding dogs, such as this border collie, are useful to farmers with cattle or sheep

"Little Lassie," the Shetland sheepdog (Sheltie), is another herding breed

WILD DOGS

Wild dogs live on every continent except Antarctica and Australia. Australia's "wild" dogs — the dingoes — are actually **domestic,** or tame, dogs that became wild again.

Several kinds of wild dogs live in North America. The largest are wolves, which are common only in parts of Alaska and Canada. A few wolves live in Idaho, Montana, Michigan, Wyoming, Minnesota and Wisconsin. Foxes and coyotes also live in North America.

Queenie is a timber wolf, and her ancestors were probably the first wild dogs to be tamed

BABY DOGS

A mother dog usually has a **litter** of two to 12 pups. The newborn pups cannot see or hear. Their eyes and ears open when they are about two weeks old.

Many dogs are full-grown when they are eight months old. Larger breeds take longer to grow up.

Most dogs live to be 13 or 14 years old. Larger breeds have shorter lives.

A golden retriever pup tackles a sponge football

HOW DOGS ARE RAISED

Pups can be taken from their mother when they are six to eight weeks old. When they are that young, pups form a friendship — or bond — with their owners.

Dogs can learn to do many things for people. Dog obedience schools train dogs to take commands. Dogs can begin training when they are six months old.

Even a breed with good herding instincts, like the Belgian Tervuren, needs to learn patience

HOW DOGS ACT

Like their wild cousins, dogs have excellent hearing and a super sense of smell. A dog's nose can lead it to food or another dog — or a person. A dog's eyesight isn't nearly as good as ours.

Farm dogs still have some of the hunting **instinct** of wild dogs. Roaming farm dogs love to chase rabbits, rats, squirrels, woodchucks, deer and other wild animals. Sometimes roaming dogs cause problems for wildlife.

Dogs "talk" with barks, whines, growls, and use "body language," such as tail-wagging.

Farm dogs love to romp with farm kids

HOW DOGS ARE USED

Most farm dogs today are family pets and friends. In the past, farm dogs were work dogs. They were trained to herd sheep and cattle.

A few farmers still use herding breeds such as collies, Belgian Tervurens and Australian shepherds to round up sheep.

Farm dogs are also useful as watch dogs. Their barking alerts farmers to visitors.

Glossary

breed (BREED) — a group or type of an animal, such as a *Saint Bernard* dog

carnivore (KAR nuh vor) — meat-eating animal, such as a dog or a cat

domestic (dum ES tihk) — referring to any of several kinds of animals tamed and raised by humans

instinct (IN stinkt) — things an animal knows how to do without being taught

litter (LIH ter) — an animal's newborn young, babies

mongrel (MAHN grul) — a dog of mixed breeds; a mutt

territory (TARE ruh tor ee) — the home area that an animal treats as its own